All About Diamonds

Discover the Fascinating World of Diamonds

Lana Frank

AuthorHouse™
1663 Liberty Drive
Bloomington, IN 47403
www.authorhouse.com
Phone: 1 (800) 839-8640

© 2016 Lana Frank. All rights reserved.

No part of this book may be reproduced, stored in a retrieval system, or
transmitted by any means without the written permission of the author.

Published by AuthorHouse 12/21/2015

ISBN: 978-1-5049-5260-6 (sc)
ISBN: 978-1-5049-5262-0 (hc)
ISBN: 978-1-5049-5261-3(e)

Library of Congress Control Number: 2015916710

Print information available on the last page.

Any people depicted in stock imagery provided by Thinkstock are models,
and such images are being used for illustrative purposes only.
Certain stock imagery © Thinkstock.

This book is printed on acid-free paper.

Because of the dynamic nature of the Internet, any web addresses or links contained in this book may have changed
since publication and may no longer be valid. The views expressed in this work are solely those of the author and do not
necessarily reflect the views of the publisher, and the publisher hereby disclaims any responsibility for them.

authorHOUSE

THIS BOOK IS DEDICATED TO MY DEAREST CHILDREN,

Tom and Chantal,

WHO ARE THE BIGGEST INSPIRATION AND GREATEST ACCOMPLISHMENT OF MY LIFE!

Contents

What is a Diamond?..1
Physical Properties of Diamonds..5
History of Diamonds...7
Formation in the Earth..10
Distribution on the Surface...12
Where Diamonds are Found...15
Mining Process...18
Rough Gem Diamonds..23
Industrials...26
Manufacturing..29
    1. Sawing...29
    2. Bruting..30
    3. Cutting..31
    4. Polishing...32
History of Diamond Cutting...33
Main Characteristics...36
    Clarity..36
    Color..37
    Cut...38
    Carat..39
Fancy-Colored Diamonds...40
Use..43
Famous Diamonds..46
Synthetic Diamonds..50
Glossary..52
Acknowledgments..55

What is a Diamond?

A diamond is a precious mineral.

The origins of the word diamond came from a Greek word "Adamas," which means "indestructible" or "invincible."

It is the hardest mineral man has ever discovered.

A diamond is the purest substance that occurs in nature.

The vast majority of diamonds are colorless. Perfectly clear stones, however, are very rare.

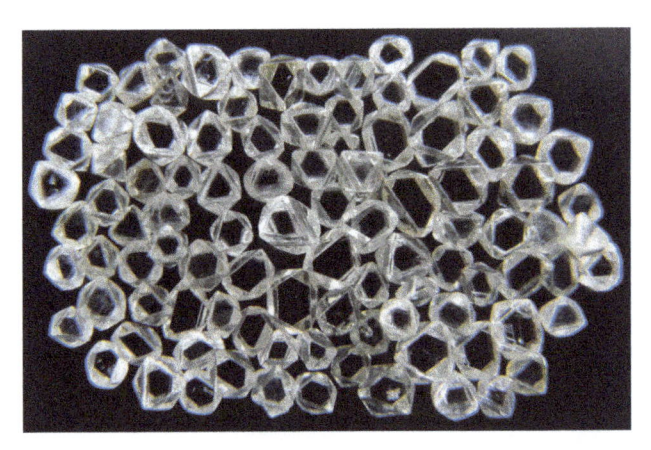

A diamond is the only transparent and colorless gemstone that has such great beauty.

Diamonds occur in every color of the rainbow.

For many centuries, diamonds have remained an absolute favorite in the world of gems and jewelry.

Initially, they were reserved for royalty and nobility, which is not the case in present time.

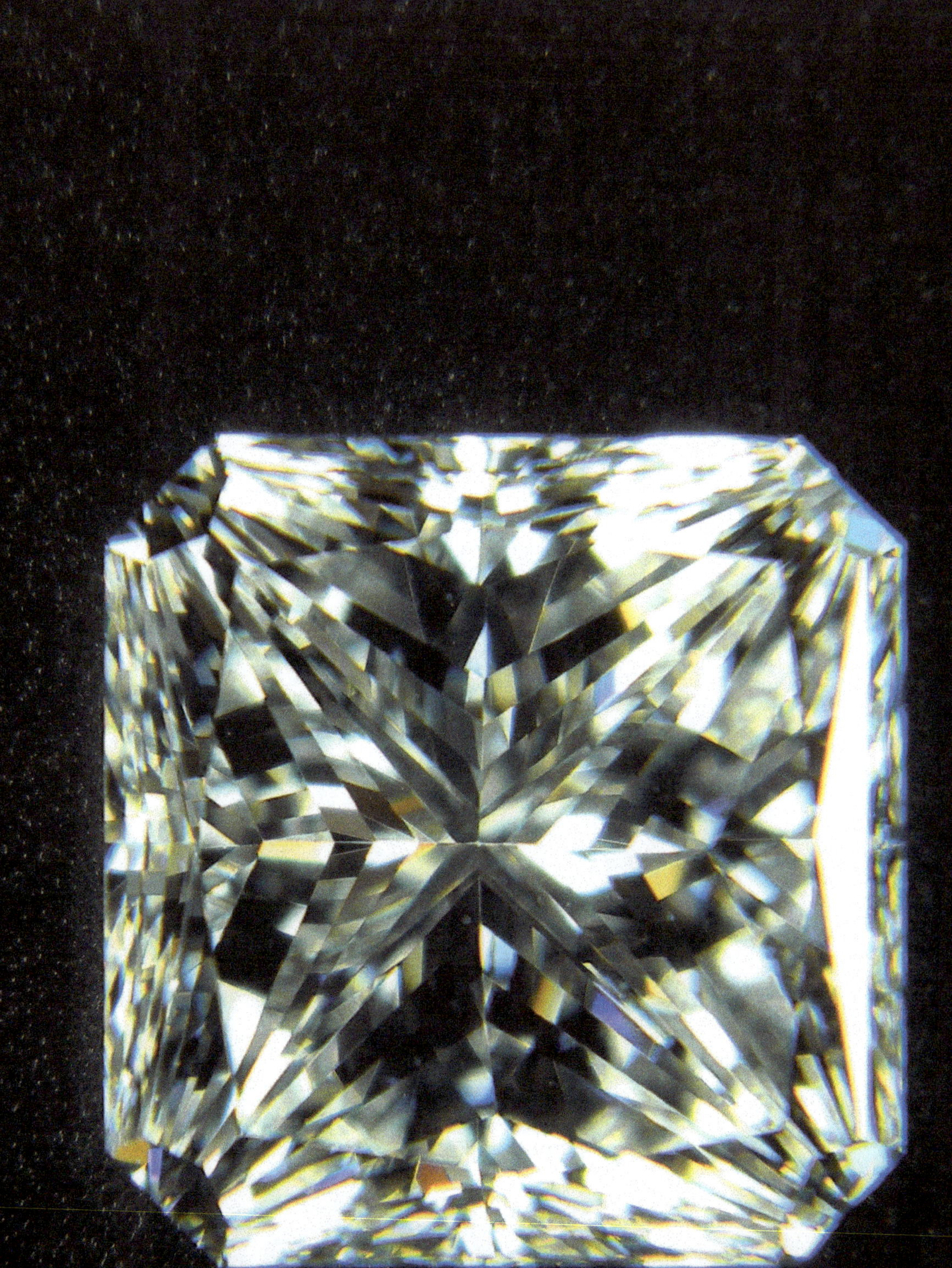

Physical Properties of Diamonds

Diamond is the only gem made of one element: carbon. Carbon is one of the Earth's most common elements, and it's found in all living things: plants, animals, and even rocks.

Carbon atoms can form diamonds or graphite, depending on the temperature and pressure. Although the atoms in diamonds and graphite are arranged differently, the carbon atoms in a diamond's crystals bond much closer together than in graphite.

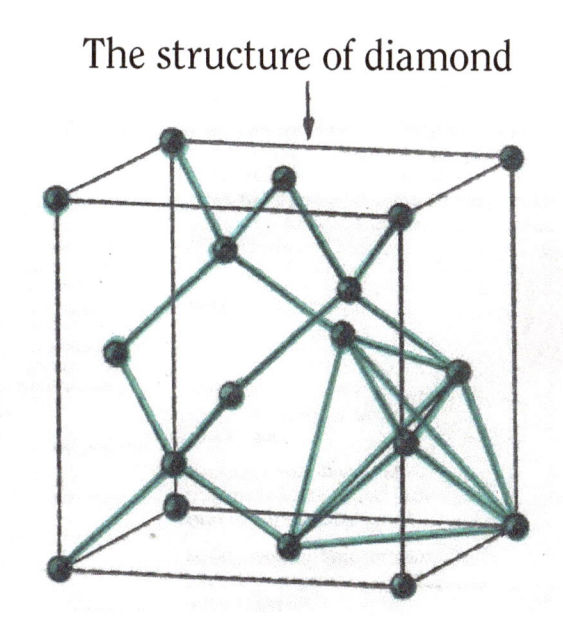

The structure of diamond

The structure of graphite

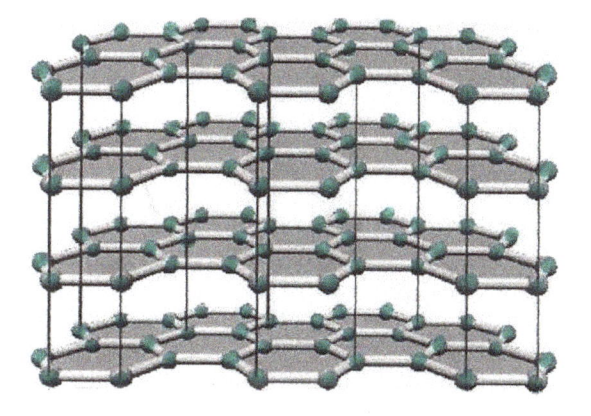

They are both from the same element, but because of the different crystal structure, graphite is one of the softest minerals whereas a diamond is the hardest natural mineral.

The exceptional hardness of a diamond reflects the ability to scratch the surface of the gem. However, diamonds are brittle when they are struck in a cleavage (grain) direction, and pieces can be broken off.

Like most minerals, diamonds have a crystal structure. Natural diamonds are found in cube, octahedron, dodecahedron, and macle crystal shapes. The most common crystal structure of a rough diamond is an octahedron.

Octahedron

Cube

Dodecahedron

Macle

History of Diamonds

Diamonds made their entrance into the world of human history in India. Thousands of years ago and by chance, man found these glass-looking pebbles (diamonds) were different from other stones. Since that time, man began to collect diamonds and treasure them. They also trade them, use them as tools, and fight over them.

The Romans treasured diamonds because of their mystical association. By the end of the Middle Ages, the cultural status of diamonds had changed. From being a mystical amulet, it became a reserve for nobility and then a fashionable jewelry stone. However, only some wealthy people were able to afford to own them.

After the great discoveries in Africa, all of that changed. Many more rough diamonds were produced than ever before, and the middle class established a new market for diamond jewelry.

The first diamond rush began in the fields of South Africa in the nineteenth century. Men of every class from almost every European nation sailed to South Africa to make a fortune. They were called "diggers." Among them were doctors, butchers, lawyers, tailors, laborers, and clerks. Hope and opportunity brought them together.

Since that time, diamonds became widespread for many other people who could afford them.

Diamonds also became the world's first hard currency.

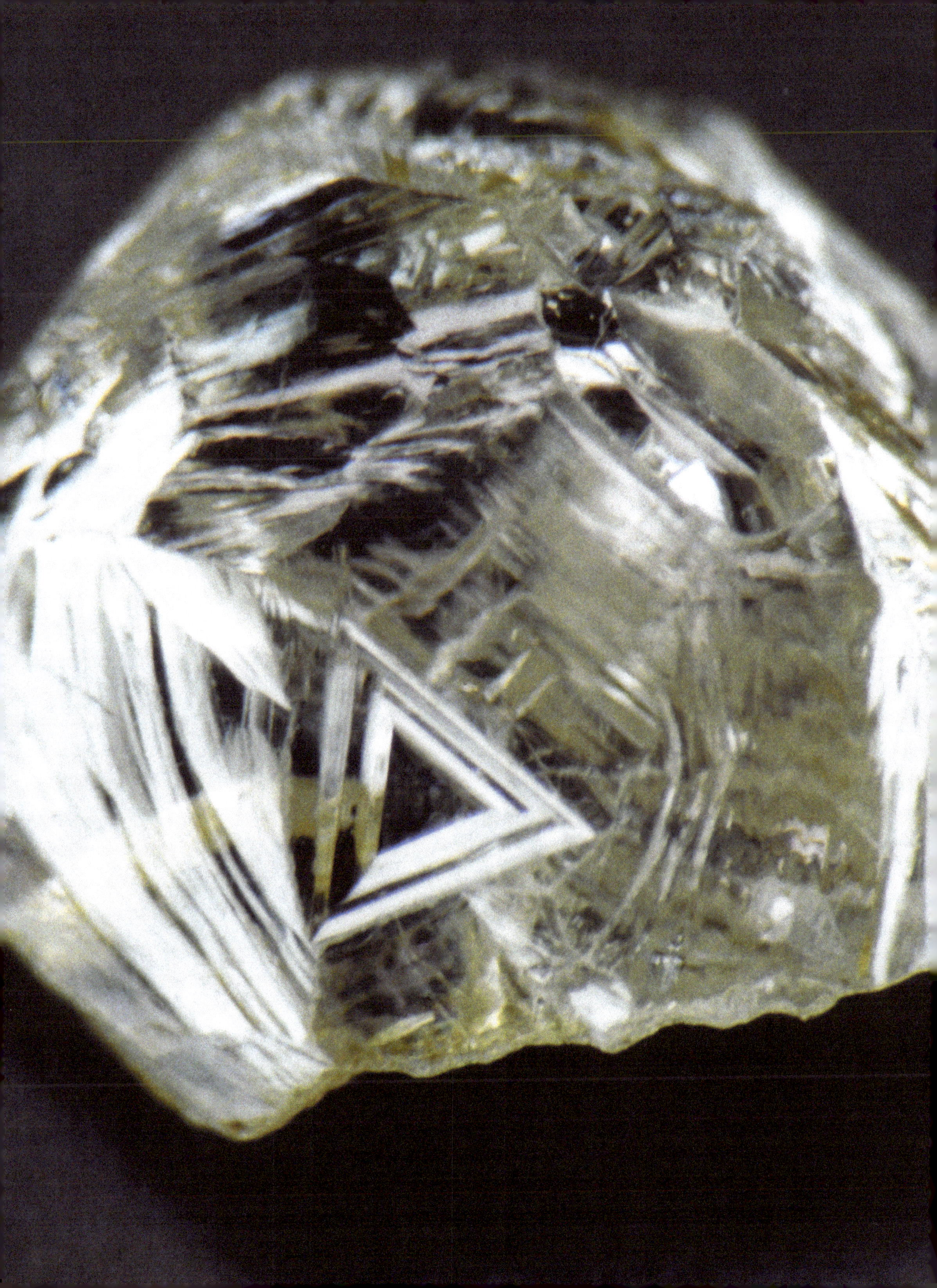

Formation in the Earth

Extreme pressure and heat, deep beneath the Earth's surface, caused the carbon atoms to crystalize and form diamonds. This occurred over a very long period of time.

Diamonds are formed much deeper in the earth than other gemstones. The process started underneath the rock plates of the continent, more than ninety miles below the Earth's surface.

Most diamonds pick up some other atoms during their growth process, but a very small percent of other atoms are detected in gem-quality diamonds.

During a volcanic eruption, as the magma flows it picks up many different rocks and minerals.

Then, kimberlite brings diamonds to the surface through the carrot-like kimberlite pipes. With the rapid drop of temperature, it becomes impossible for diamonds to transform to graphite.

The term "natural diamond" means this mineral came from nature.

Distribution on the Surface

Diamonds are delivered to the Earth's surface by volcanic eruption. The first delivery came approximately 2.5 billion years ago.

Although kimberlite pipes have been discovered all over the world, most of them do not contain diamonds. Only about thirty of the 6,000 volcanic pipes have become major diamond pipes. Only about 1 percent of kimberlite deposits contain enough diamonds to make them valuable.

Any new pipes have to be studied carefully for their ability to produce before mining begins.

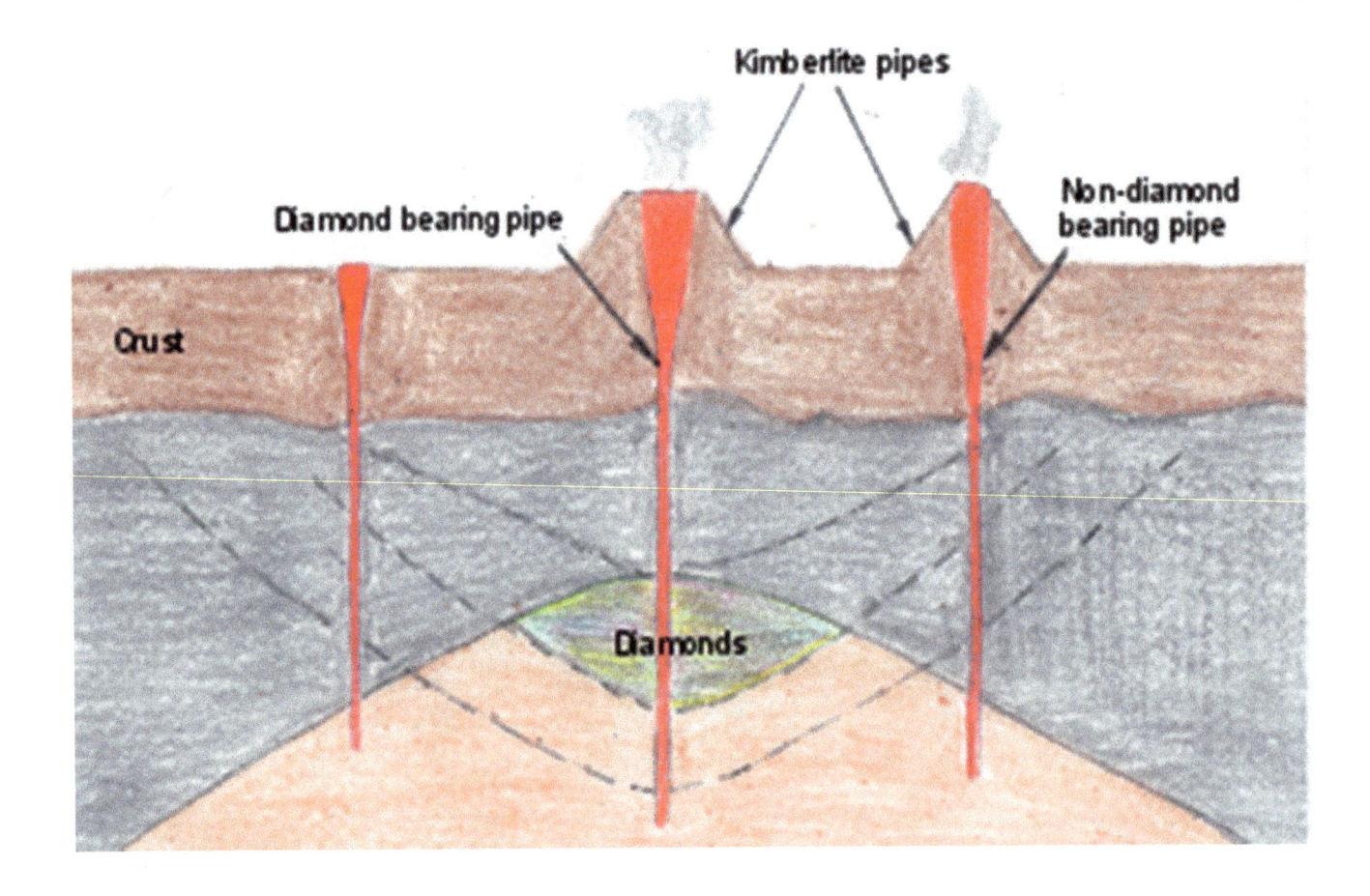

Kimberlite pipes are not the only source of diamonds. In fact, approximately 80 percent of all diamonds mined come from underground pipes. About 20 percent come from alluvial sources, such are rivers and streams. Water carries the diamond-bearing gravels from short to long distances, even into the sea.

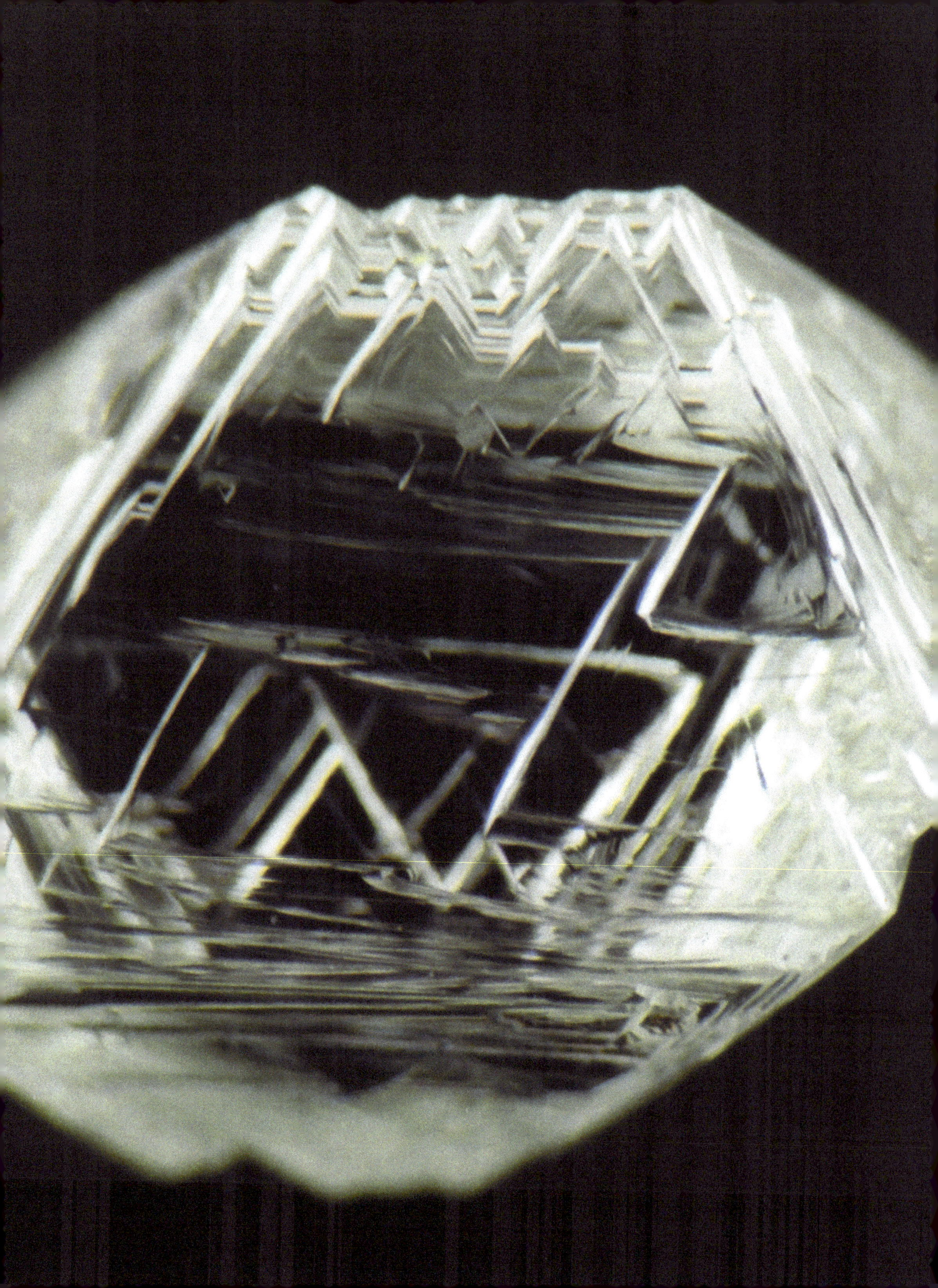

Where Diamonds are Found

Diamonds were first found in India before 500 B.C., and, for many centuries, India was the only place where diamonds were mined.

They were discovered by chance while mining for gold. The deposits in India were rich enough to supply most of the world's diamonds until the eighteenth century.

At the same time (eighteenth century), diamonds were discovered in Brazil in the gravel of rivers.

As the supply of diamonds was running out in Brazil, huge deposits were found in Africa in the 1860s. Soon, it became the chief source in the world.

Later, in 1953, huge diamond fields were discovered in Siberia, Russia. This made Russia the second-largest producer of diamonds in the world at that time.

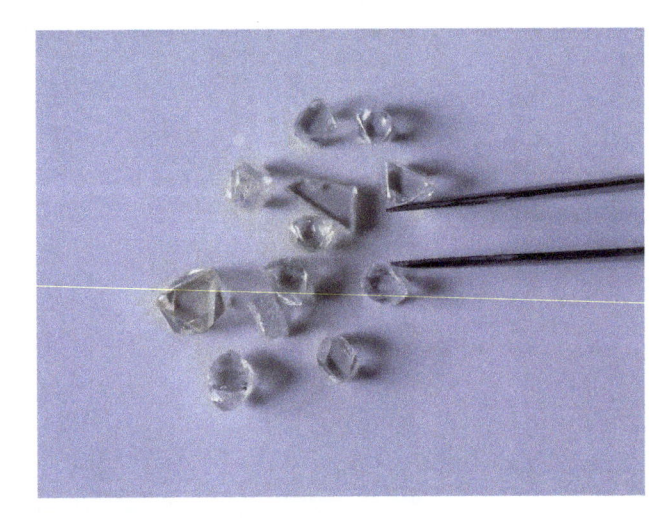

In 1906, small deposits of diamonds were found in Arkansas, USA. Today, the diamond mine is owned and operates by the state government.

Considerable quantities have been discovered in China and Australia.

The newest place in the world for diamond mining is Western Canada.

Today, diamonds are found on every continent, but in different qualities and quantities. Even so, Africa is still the world's leader in the production of rough diamonds.

In the past, new diamond sources were discovered by accident only. Now, with more knowledge and available technology, the search for diamond deposits has improved.

Mining Process

Diamond mining is a complex process. To produce one carat of rough diamond, tons of rocks and sand have to be moved and processed.

Nearly all diamond sources are found in remote places of the world. Some of them are located in very harsh climate conditions. An example would be Siberia and the Kalahari desert.

As you have learned, rough diamonds are found in two types of deposits:

1. Primary deposits, such as kimberlite pipes (the remains of ancient volcanoes which originally brought them to the surface);

2. Secondary deposits, such as alluvial rivers, streams, and even oceans. Sometimes found thousands of miles from their source, they were first brought to the surface of the Earth.

For a long time, diamonds were mined from the sand and gravel of surrounding rivers. Much later in Africa, in 1870, diamonds were found in the earth from the river source. Since then, dry digging for diamonds was born.

Underground mining is a more difficult procedure. Every day, miners move tons of blue ground to be processed to extract the diamonds. As pipes get deeper, they become more narrow and the yield becomes less. Eventually, the mine is shut down.

In many parts of the world, alluvial diamonds are mined with the simplest equipment that was used by miners hundreds of years ago: shovels, wide shallow pans, and picks.

About 250 tons of rock must be mined and processed to produce one carat of gem-quality diamond. This is what makes them so valuable and unique.

With sophisticated and automatic equipment, diamonds can be sorted out.

Still, in the last stage of the mining process, diamonds have to be sorted by hand. There is no substitute for the human brain, eye, and hand.

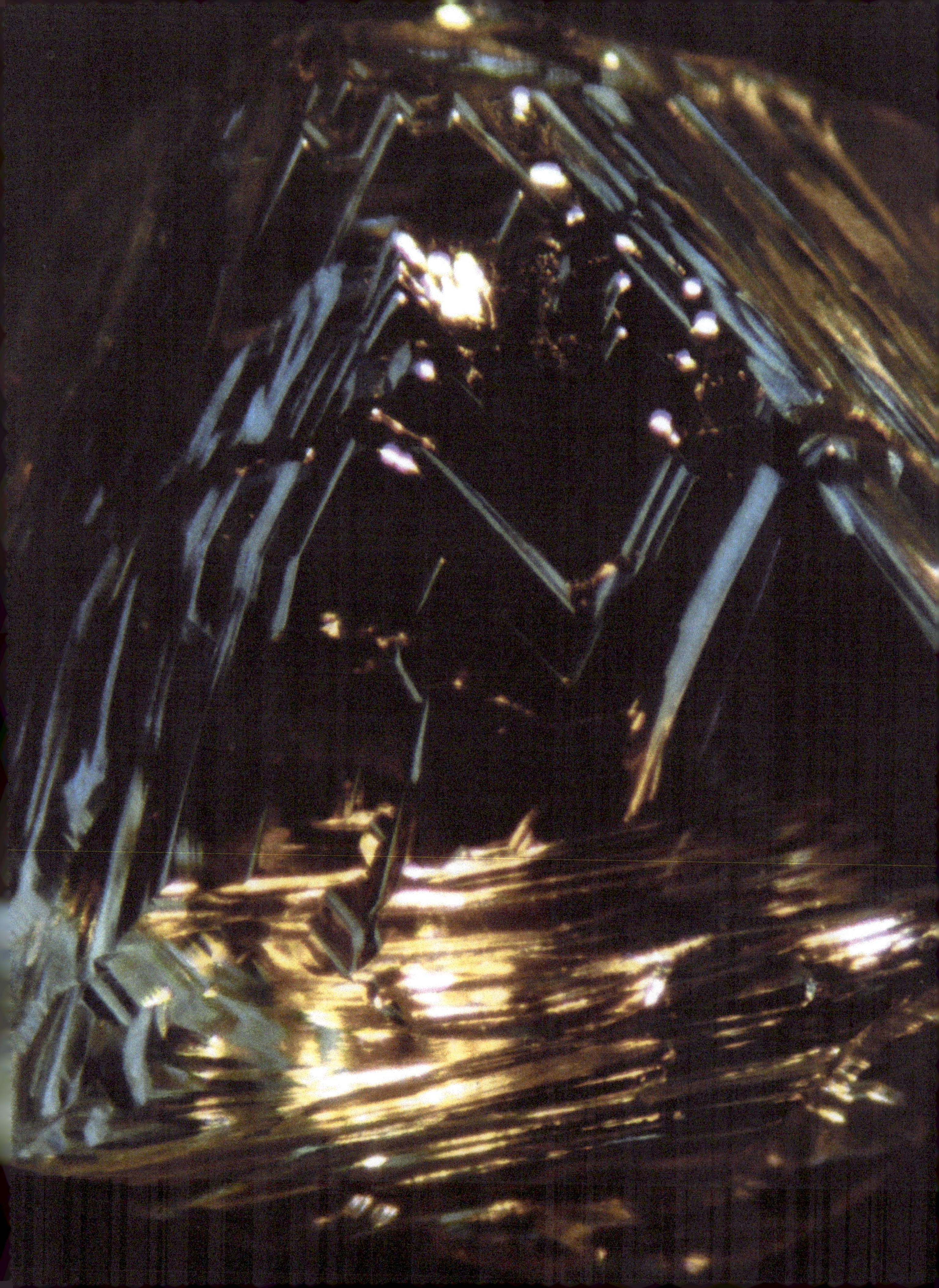

Rough Gem Diamonds

Rough diamonds are when they are still in natural form and have not been cut or polished.

All rough diamonds can be divided into the following groups:

1. Gem-quality diamonds

2. Industrial-quality diamonds

First, when rough diamonds are found, they look a lot like glass pebbles.

Diamonds that are extracted from different areas include different trace element. Nature gives each rough diamond unique characteristics.

Some diamonds have a frosted surface. This is a common for rough diamonds found in riverbed deposits.

All rough diamonds have some distinguishing marks, known as inclusions, which make each one unique.

When diamonds are mined, small gems are discovered much more frequently than large ones. That's what it makes large diamonds much more valuable. Good quality rough diamonds get a lot of attention.

After rough gem diamonds are mined, they have to be sorted, graded, and priced.

Only when a rough crystal reaches the hands of a cutter is the real internal beauty of a diamond revealed.

Industrials

Industrials are very low quality diamonds that are not suitable as gems.

The differences between industrial and gem diamonds are determined by the environment they form in. If the crystals were formed relatively large and clean, the result is gem diamonds. If the crystals have a high concentration of impurities, the result is industrial diamonds.

The exceptional hardness of diamonds plays an important role in modern industrial technology. About 80 percent of diamonds that are mined are for industrial use.

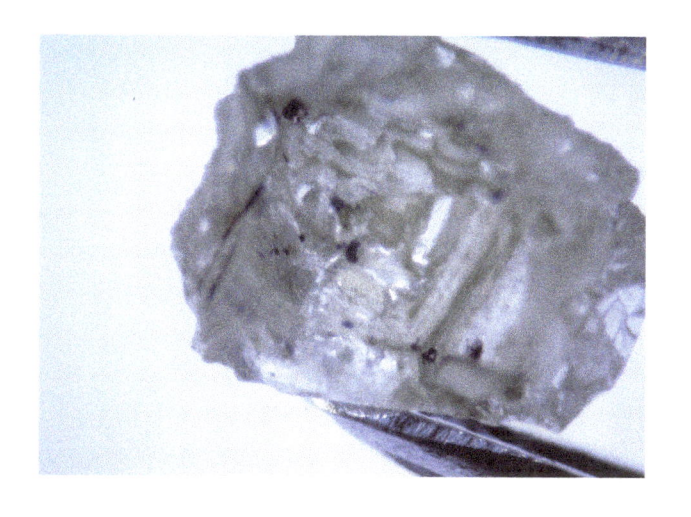

The annual demand for industrial rough diamonds is approximately 90 to 150 million carats. A large part of this demand is met by synthetic diamonds.

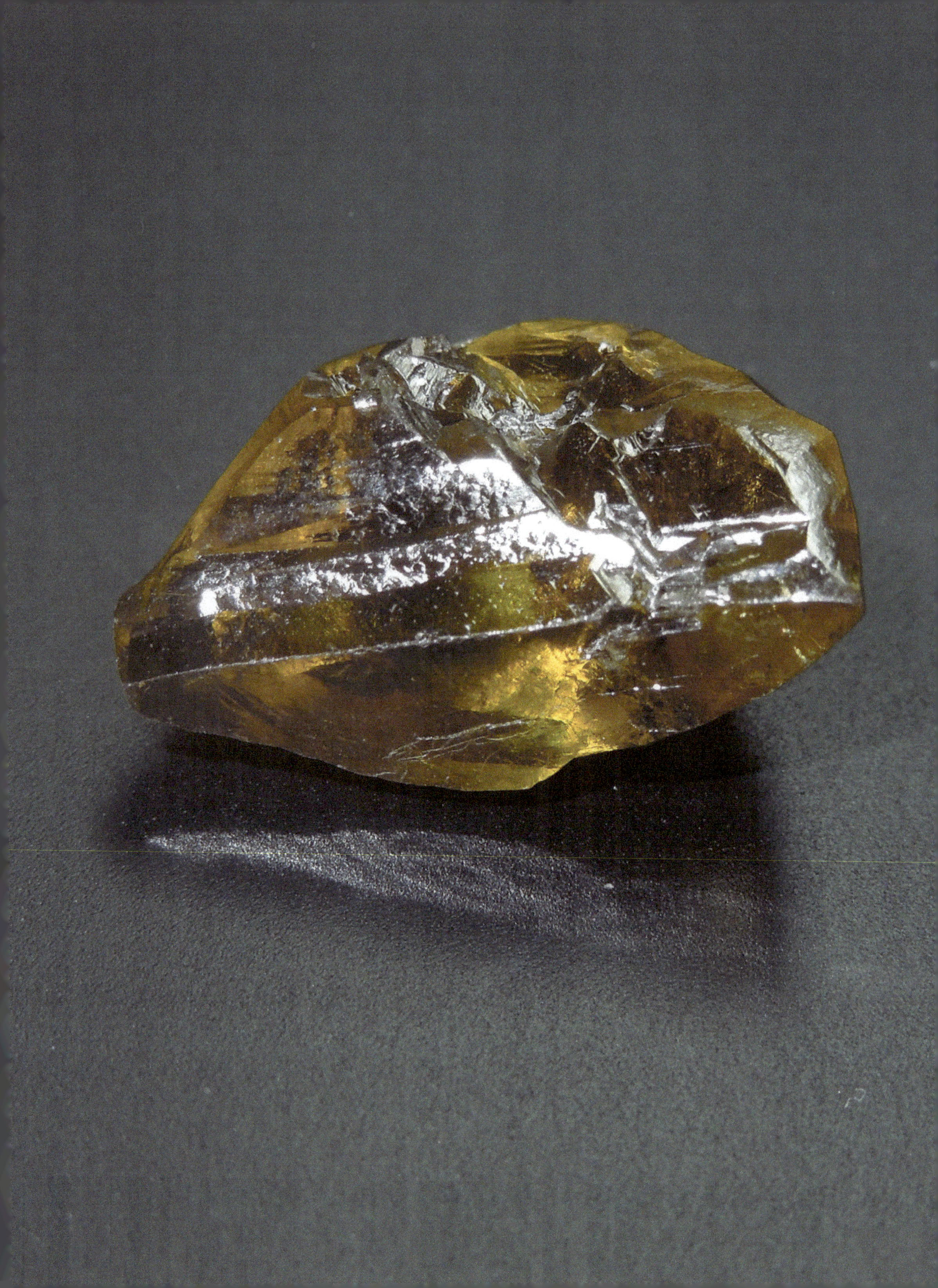

Manufacturing

Manufacturing a gem diamond is accomplished in four basic stages:

>Step 1: Sawing
>Step 2: Bruting
>Step 3: Cutting
>Step 4: Polishing

1. Sawing

   Sawing is dividing (slicing) a crystal. It can be done by conventional sawing with a special metal disc covered with diamond powder on a blade. It is a slow operation. A one-carat diamond can take from two to four or more hours, depending on the size and shape of the stone and difficulties during sawing.

   Sawing also can be done by a laser. Laser technology reduces the sawing time by 50 percent at least.

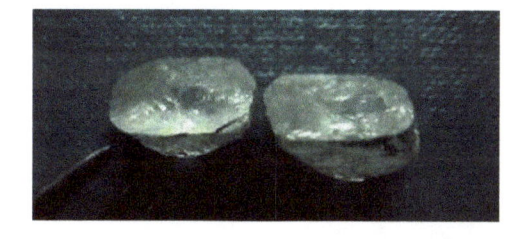

2. Bruting

The process of rounding the corners of a diamond is known as bruting. It can be done by rotating a gem diamond against an industrial that is held in a fixed position.

Essentially, one diamond is used to shape the other.

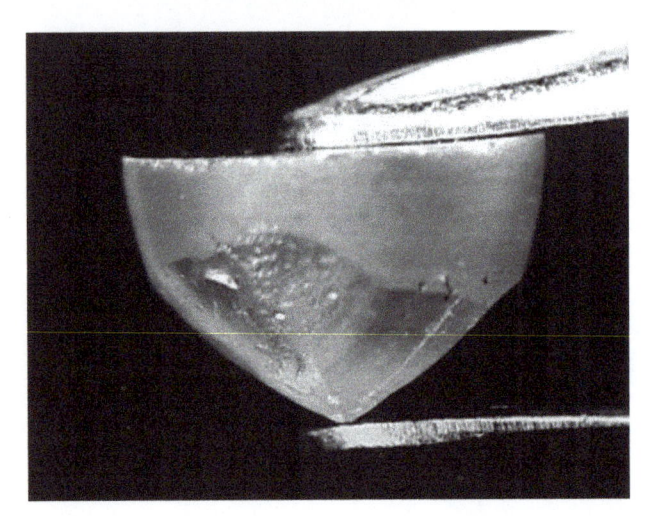

3. Cutting

The cut of a diamond is its shape after it's done. The cut of a diamond is extremely important in determing the brilliance within the diamond. In other words, if a diamond has a poor cut, it will appear dull, even if it has perfect clarity and color.

The major factor of the diamond cut is its proportions. The maximum light reflection is given to the stone when it has the perfect proportions of each facet.

Another important aspect of the cutting process is symmetry. This refers to the alignment of the facets. After the rough diamond is cut and polished, it loses about 50 percent of its weight.

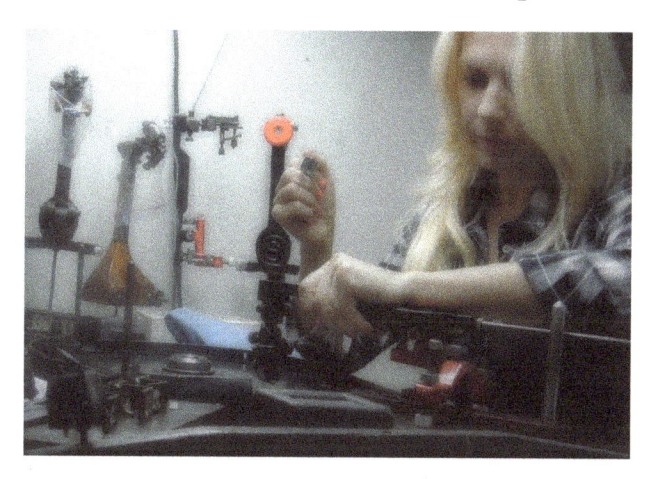

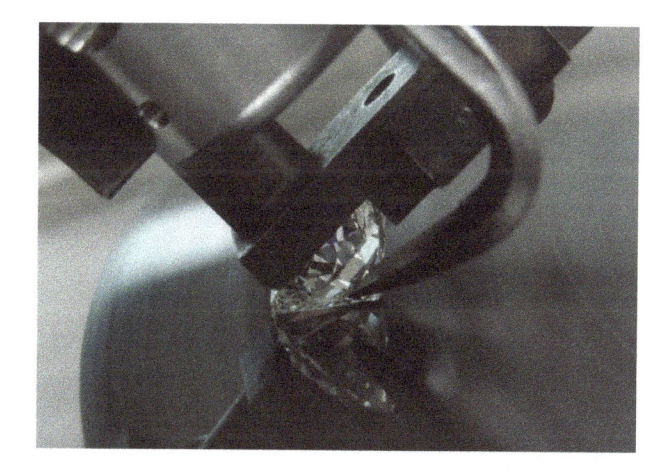

4. Polishing

Polishing is the final stage in the manufacturing process of a gem diamond. It can be done on a flat, metal wheel to which diamond powder is bonded. Only a diamond can cut a diamond.

When gems are polished, the surface is not abraded. A poorly polished diamond has a blurred and minimum sparkle.

Diamonds, because of their hardness, will take and keep the best polish much better than any other gemstone.

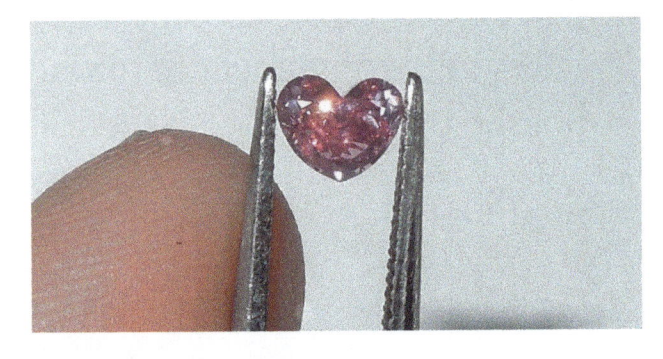

History of Diamond Cutting

Centuries ago, when diamonds were used as talisman only, they were not shaped and polished, but placed in rings in natural form. It's assumed that the first faceted diamond came from India, probably during the fourteenth century.

The history of diamond cutting and polishing is poorly documented, and it remains a trade secret for many centuries. Today, there are cutting centers all over the world. The main centers are in India, Belgium, Israel, and South Africa.

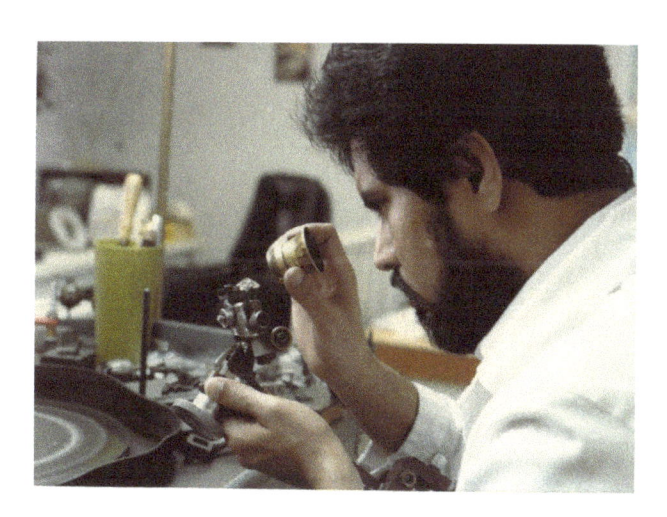

A skilled cutter can maximize the beauty and value of each diamond by cutting and polishing with precise accuracy. Each stage of the diamond cutting process determines the quality of the final stone. It can take days or even weeks of work.

It took many centuries to develop modern cutting styles and techniques. The real beauty of a diamond is fully revealed only after it is cut and polished. Cut is the greatest human influence on a diamond's beauty.

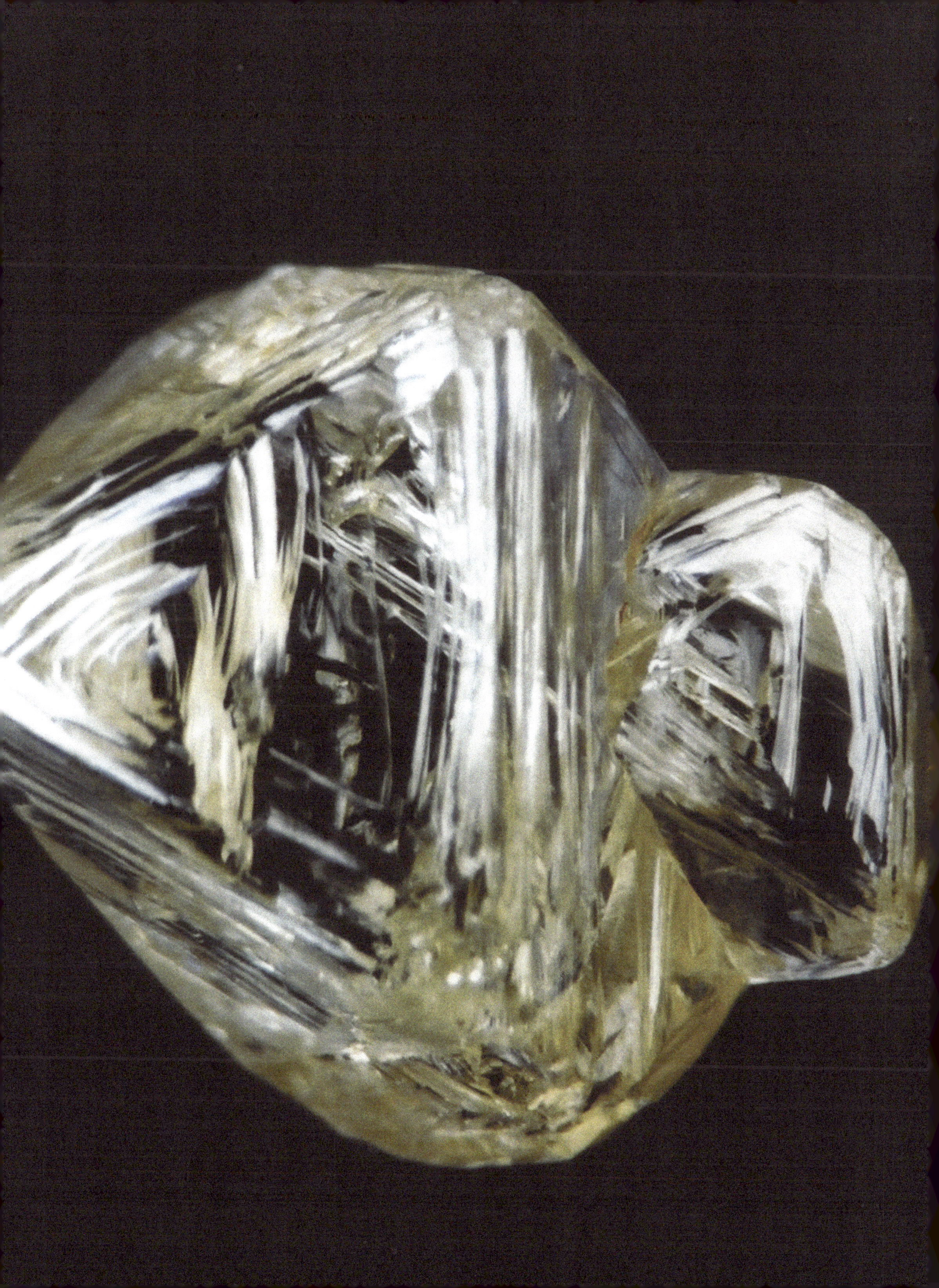

Main Characteristics

The value of a polished diamond is based on the four C's. These characteristics are:

- Clarity
- Color
- Cut
- Carat

Clarity

The term clarity is based on its purity. The purity of a diamond affects its quality and therefore its price. Diamonds can range from flawless to heavily flawed.

Diamonds that are absolutely clear are the most rare and most expensive. However, the majority of diamonds have internal and external inclusions, such as scratches and other minerals. Sometime they are visible only under the microscope. Almost all diamonds possess some type of inclusion.

Color

Diamonds are found in a wide range of colors. Any of these colors can occur in various degree intensities.

Diamonds can be green, blue, black, red, purple, pink, brown, and orange. The white-to-yellow range of colors is the largest group found in gem diamonds. Diamonds with a pure, single, vivid color are extremely rare.

Color is of major importance in gem diamonds, but not in industrial ones.

Cut

The cut of the diamond is its shape after being manufactured. The common cuts are: brilliant (round shape), princess (square shape), emerald (rectangle shape), and marquise. Each shape has its beauty and is a matter of personal taste.

Diamonds are also found on the market with unusual or specially designed cuts. Almost any cutting style can be attractive. Proportions are the key. The cut is the only factor of a diamond's value that is controlled by human hands.

The most popular cut is the 58-facet round brilliant.

Carat

Diamonds and other gemstones are measured by the carat. A carat is a very old unit of weight. It was established in the early twentieth century. One carat equals 0.2 grams.

The carat reflects a diamond's size. The greater the weight of a stone, the higher the price per carat.

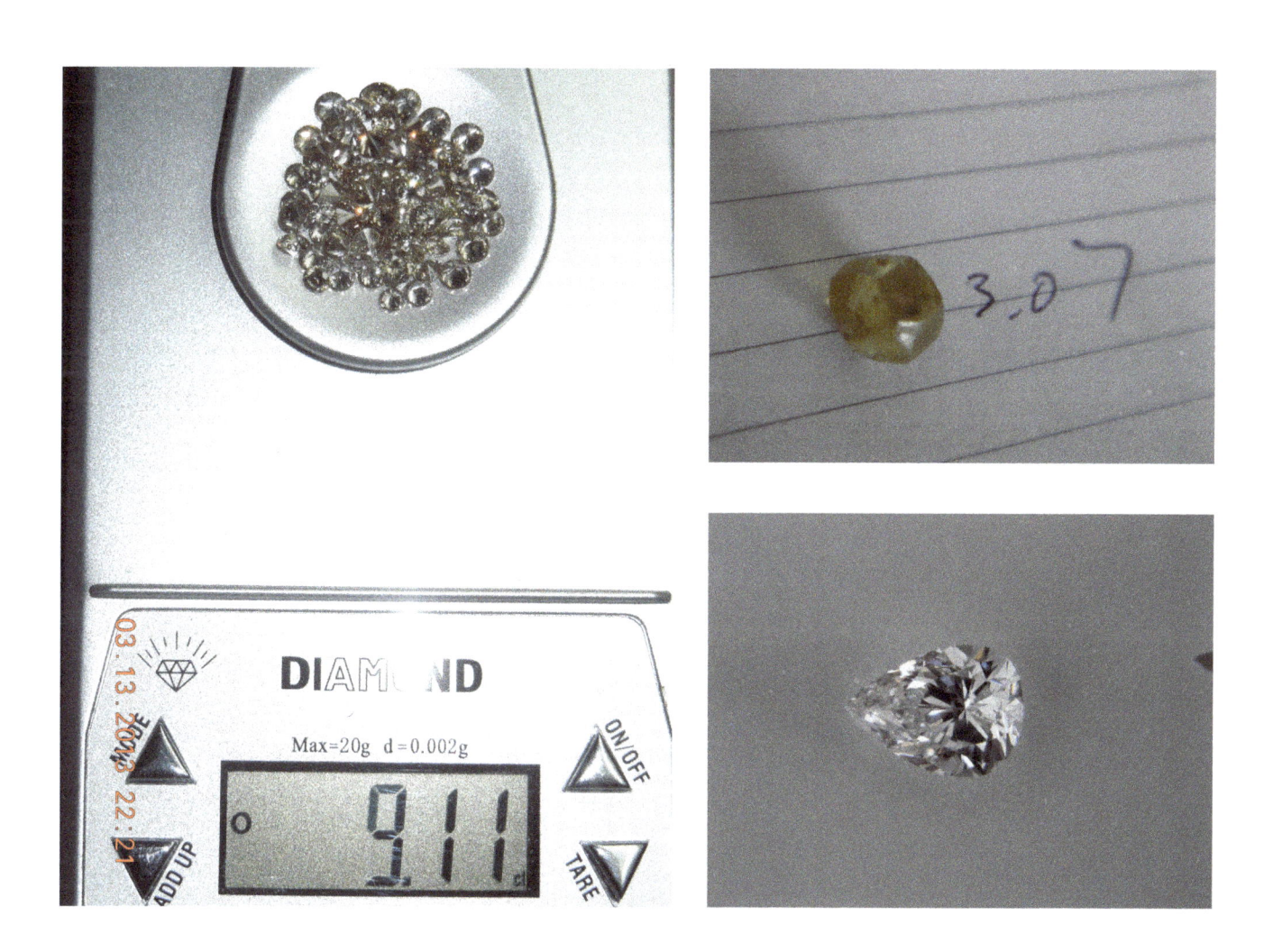

Fancy-Colored Diamonds

When a color is very bright and deep in a diamond, it is called a fancy. These colors are rare and have a high value. Approximately one in every 10,000 diamonds has a natural fancy color.

Colors in diamonds are caused by structural distortions and chemical impurities. Brown, red, and pink colors in diamonds are caused by distortions in the crystal structure. Green colors are caused by natural radiation, when diamond comes in contact with radioactive rocks. The combination of both chemical impurities and structural distortion leads to other colors.

The majority of fancy-colored diamonds is not intense and pure. Usually, they are modified with other colors, such as gray or yellow. This means that larger fancy-colored diamonds are extremely rare.

The most common fancy colors are brown and light yellows. Reds, blues, and greens are some of the rarest fancy colors.

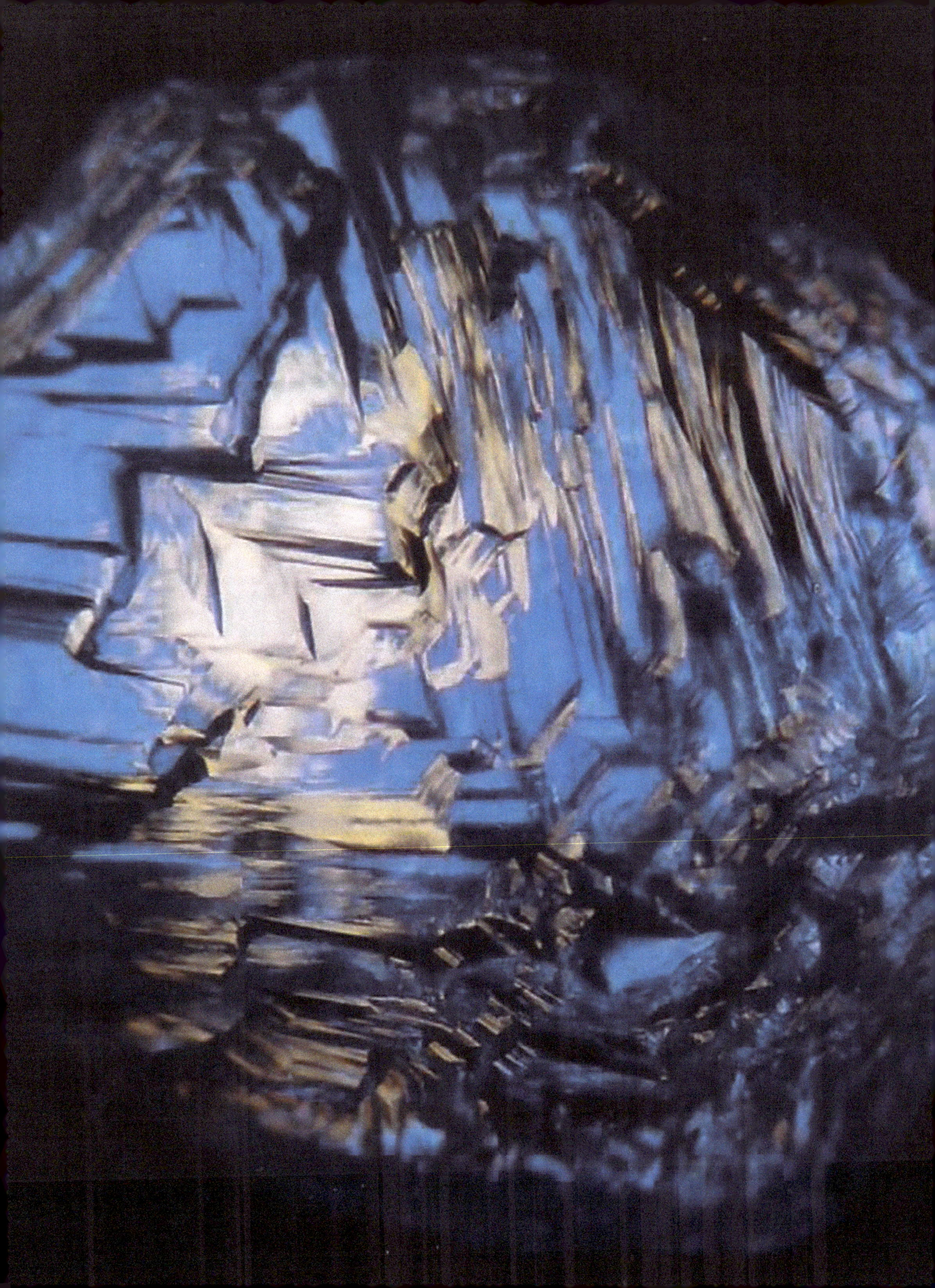

Use

Diamonds have many uses. They have attracted man's attention for thousands of years.

In the past, diamonds were used as a talisman. From the earliest days until comparatively recent times, some people believed in the spiritual power of diamonds: to cure diseases, protect from evil spirits, healing, happiness, and even poisoning.

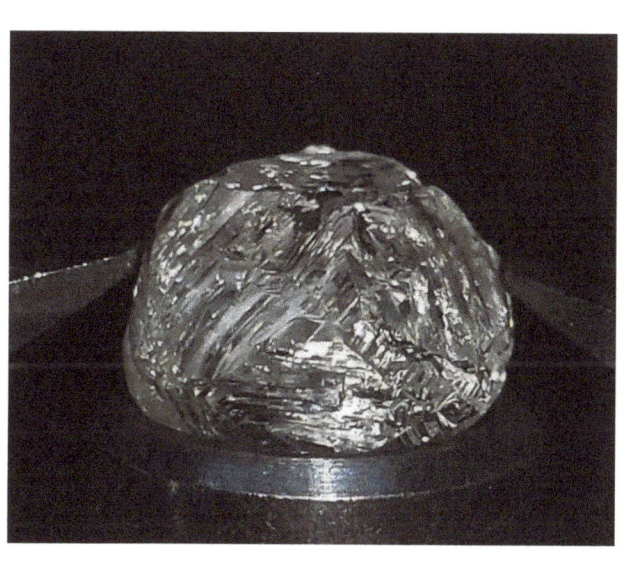

Today, a diamond of great beauty is available for people to buy, unlike the ancient Roman nobles who had to settle for rough crystal in their times.

About 20 percent of rough diamonds that are mined are used for jewelry and adornments, mainly in rings, earrings, pendants, watches, and brooches.

After many years of constant wear, polished diamonds will preserve their corners and sharp edges when most other stones will have become worn and chipped.

About two million carats of cut diamonds are used in the market each year.

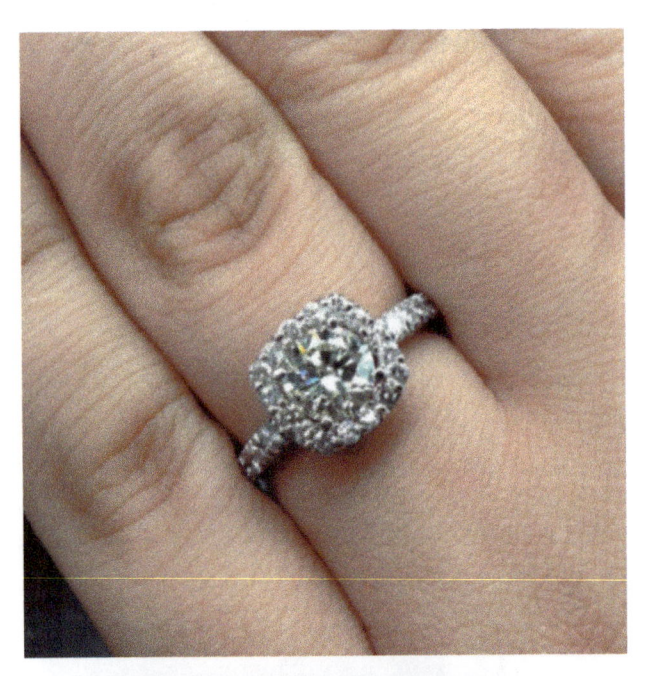

The diamond is the birthstone for April. Some people believe that wearing a gem of their birth month will bring them luck.

The other 80 percent of diamonds are used for industrial. These uses include: surgical tools, grinding wheels, videodisc needles, cutting tools, dentist drills, sophisticated electronic equipment, and many others.

Famous Diamonds

Some diamonds are famous due to their exceptional size, color, and quality. Most of them have an interesting and complex history.

The largest diamond crystal ever found is named the Cullinan diamond. It weighed 3,106 carats in the rough, with very high quality and purity. It was found in South Africa in 1905. It was divided into nine major stones, ninety-six small stones, and almost ten carats in remains.

The largest stone from it was the Cullinan 1, or the Star of Africa. It's the largest cut diamond in the world, and its weight is 530.20 carats.

This pear-shaped diamond is set in the Royal Scepter and kept in the Tower of London with other crown jewels.

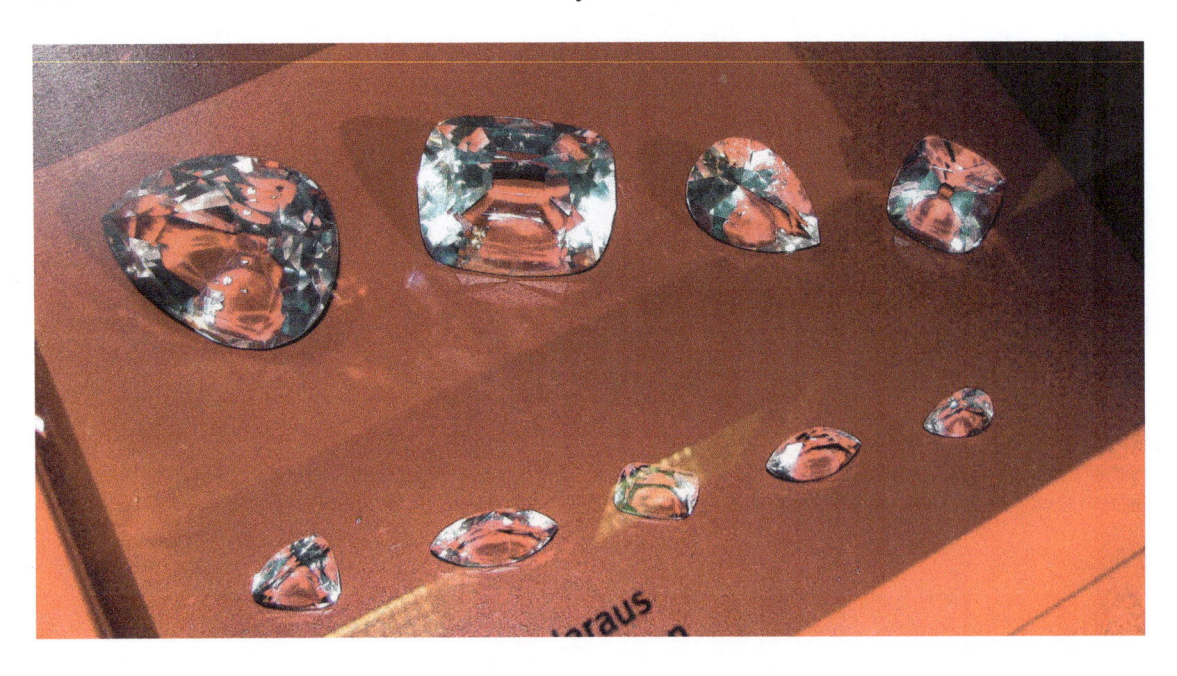

The Hope diamond was found in the seventeenth century (1642) near India and weights 112 carats in the rough. The Hope diamond has a fine, deep blue color. In 1958, the Hope diamond was presented to the Museum of Natural History in Washington, D.C. The weight of the cut diamond is 45.52 carats. It was once owned by Louis XVI and Marie Antoinette.

The Koh-i-Nur diamond has the largest history of all the famous diamonds. It is also called the Mountain of Light and weighs 191 carats. It was found in India in 1304. Today, it is a part of the English Crown Jewels.

The **Orloff** (sometime spelt Orlov) diamond was found in India, at the beginning of the seventeenth century. It is one of the world's most historic diamonds with a weight of 300 carats in the rough. Presently it is on exhibition in the Diamond Treasury of Russia in Moscow.

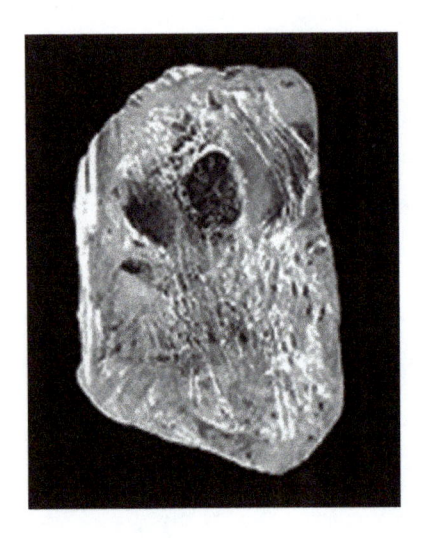

The **Star of Sierra Leone** is the largest alluvial diamond ever discovered. It was picked out of the separator plant at a mine in Sierra Leone. It is one of the highest gem quality diamonds in the world. The weight was 969 carats in the rough. This enormous colorless crystal was cut into seventeen stones.

The **Excelsior** diamond was discovered in South Africa in 1893. It was a high clarity blue-white stone with an irregular shape. Its rough weight was 971 carats.

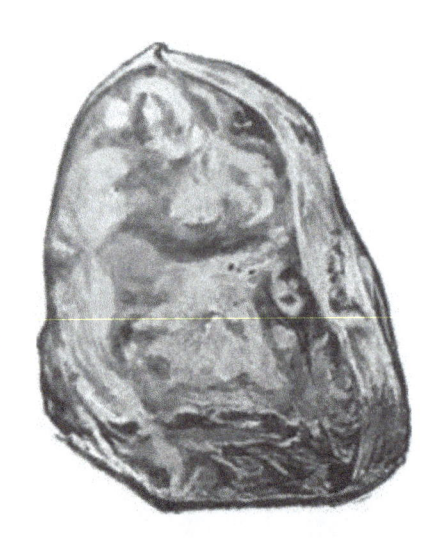

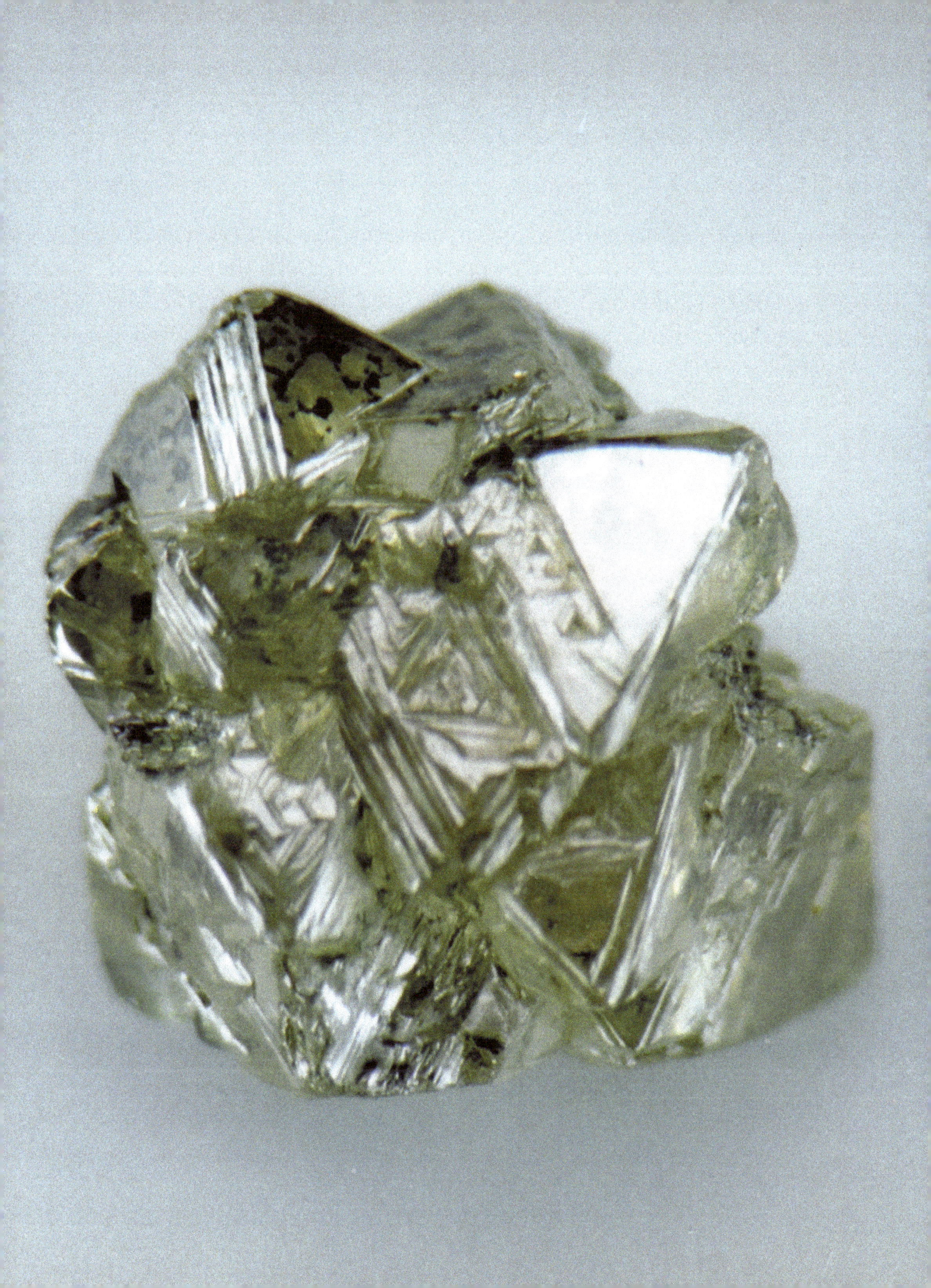

Synthetic Diamonds

What is synthetic diamond? It's a diamond made in a factory (laboratory-grown diamond). A synthetic diamond is made of exactly the same material as a natural one: carbon atoms. Sometimes it is difficult to see the difference. A laboratory can determine whether a stone is natural or synthetic.

A diamond that is unnatural means that minerals were created by human technology, and not by nature.

The first synthetic diamonds were produced in 1954.

Synthetic diamonds are produced in the laboratory by compressing carbon to extreme temperatures and pressures. They are made in a short time and do not remain in high temperatures and pressures for long periods of time.

Many synthetic diamonds are manufactured each year. Still, they are not a threat to natural gem diamonds.

Both synthetic gem-quality diamonds and synthetic industrial diamonds are manufactured for many different uses. They are both commercially important.

Gem-quality synthetic diamonds became useful in the jewelry industry, and more than 100 million carats of industrial diamonds are produced every year.

Glossary

Here are the meanings of some words that are useful to know when learning about diamonds.

ALLUVIAL: a soil left by rivers or floods

BLUE GROUND: a layer of kimberlite

BRUTING: to shape a diamond into a round(ish) shape

CARAT: a unit of measurement. One carat equals 200 milligram, or 0.20 of a grams

CARBON: a chemical element that is found in all living things

CRYSTAL: a solid substance that forms particular types of minerals

CUT: the shape into which a rough stone is cut and polished

DIAMOND: a very hard gemstone

DIAMOND CUTTER: a person who transforms a rough diamond by cutting and polishing it into a fully faceted gem

FACET: one of the flat surfaces of a cut diamond

GEMSTONE: a valuable stone, suitable for jewelry

GRAPHITE: a mineral, soft black substance

INDUSTRIALS: "low quality" diamonds

KIMBERLITE: volcanic rock

KIMBERLITE PIPES: volcanic pipes, the source of diamonds

MAGMA: molten rock inside the earth

MINERAL: a natural substance in the earth with very specific characteristics, such as hardness

MINING: the extraction of materials such as minerals from the earth

POLISHING: a process that makes a diamond reflect light

RIVERBED: the bottom of a river

ROUGH: the name given to crystals of diamonds as they are mined, before the cut. It is used as in "rough diamond" or just "rough"

SAWING: the separation of diamond into separate pieces

Forever You Photography

Thank you for buying this book!

About the Author

Lana Frank is an accomplished diamond cutter with over ten years of experience and is the founder of Diamond Faceting, Inc. She has focused on cutting and polishing rough diamonds and recutting old-mine cut diamonds to modern proportions. Ms. Frank is considered a specialist in fancy-colored diamonds and rough diamonds. She published her previous children's book DIAMONDS in 2012.

Website: www.diamondfaceting.com
Email: diamondfaceting@usa.com

Acknowledgments

I would like to thank my daughter Chantal Peters, age eight, for providing amazing drawings for this book and for her valuable advice in regards to the layout of the pages.

Photo credits

1. American Institute of Diamond Cutting

2. Mr. Edmond Blackford

3. Apollo Synthetic Diamond image found on page 50-51 by Steve Jurvetson (http://www.flickr.com/photos/jurvetson/156830367/) [CC BY 2.0 (http://creativecommons.org/licenses/by/2.0)], via Wikimedia Commons

CPSIA information can be obtained
at www.ICGtesting.com
Printed in the USA
LVHW070114080321
680832LV00023B/1308